Living
With
Ghosts

True Tales of the Paranormal

Dorothy Burtz Fiedel

Printed in the United States of America
Science Press
300 W. Chestnut Street
Ephrata, Pa 17522
Published by Dorothy Burtz Fiedel
All Photos by Dorothy Burtz Fiedel unless otherwise
indicated.

ISBN 0-9640254- 3-4

Cover Photo – Is it sunrise or sunset over the Caribbean? This
photo was taken by Justin S. Dickinson from the deck of the
Navy destroyer, the U.S.S. Arthur W. Radford, somewhere in
the Caribbean Ocean off the coast of Saint Croix. December
1998.

To My Beloved Husband

Samuel Solomon Fiedel

1916 – 1998

As melodies of memory
Linger, circle, round my head
Our waltz of life so sweet, so brief
Some say, has reached its end

But death just twirls to a minor chord
Suspended as weightless dew,
It hovers aloft as a note unresolved
And echoes reflections of you

I now patiently sit on the dais of life,
And wait for the grand maestro's cue
Dance slippers I keep, to slide on my feet
For I've saved the last waltz for you.

Dottie

TABLE OF CONTENTS

THE PROMISE

This book is the fulfillment of a promise I made to my beloved husband Sam, as he lay on his deathbed. The cancer, which he had so valiantly fought, was winning. It was now leukemia and pneumonia that joined hands and transformed into a powerful foe, resistant to medicine, resistant to hope and tears and prayers.

On at least 10 separate occasions during the last 31 days of his life, he brought up the subject of a fourth book. It was only after I would verbally say, "Yes, I promise I'll write it," that he gazed at me through weary eyes and sighed, a look of relief softening his brow, as if my answer was the solution to all of our problems.

He insisted I start writing immediately after his death and promised he would provide me with 'material'.

Sam kept his word…

ALPHA AND OMEGA

"No thought exists in me which death
has not carved with his chisel."
Michelangelo[1]

T he business of ghosts and hauntings is totally and inescapably linked with the business of death. I am sad to write that death is one of the driving forces behind this book.

Since the recent death of my beloved husband Sam in March of 1998, I have churned the strange events surrounding his passing over and over in my mind.

The urgency I have felt to tell others about a strange and wondrous phenomenon I experienced, has nipped at my heels, and tugged at my clothing. It has rolled over my mind as surf in a storm. For months and months, this urgency dogged me as I delayed putting the event into words to be read by the public.

Some might suggest that I am a widow seeking catharsis. No, I am not.

I might be criticized for writing so candidly about an event so personal, or chastised that I threw propriety out the window at the expense of one so dear, one so respected, one so missed; but this book was the last thing my husband asked of me. I am bound by love and honor to see his wish fulfilled; my promise kept.

It just so happens that I write about ghosts. The true accounts I collect come from people from all occupations, varied religious beliefs, and different geographic locations. Perhaps these true events just might suggest, and ultimately, might offer tangible proof, or at least hope, that there is survival after death.

Possibly, one question has darted through the thinking, reasoning, mind of every individual, at least once in his lifetime: What happens to us after we die?

Do our bodies just shut down, immediately transforming us into a heap of useless, decaying matter? Do our minds flicker as the power supply is yanked, the screen of our mind going black, never to flicker to life again? Nothingness? Silence?

Power supply? Think about it. What is plugged into what? What is the spark that animates man?

Our brain is a super computer fuelled by chemical reactions and electrical interaction between countless biological cells. As we float in our developmental bubble of the womb, how, when, and by what, is our mind jolted into operation? How long are the jumper cables for life; and who holds the ends?

While I was a college student, I once listened as a philosophy professor gave his explanation as to why people did not like to go to funerals. According to this intelligent man, the reason for our dislike of funerals was that everyone who viewed the dead was scared stiff that they would find themselves as the next occupant of the box. For the professor, death was the cessation of everything and nothing existed after the moment of death.

Sadly, I often thought he must find his philosophical contemplation an ultimately, intellectually, useless practice. His fear, whether rational or not, must at times be all consuming for like it or not, death is inevitable. If one is born, then there is a time one must die.

His view of death, in my opinion, would make the pursuit of philosophical questions of "being" a hopeless endeavor. However, in defense of my college professor, my opinion may not be totally accurate. Take into consideration that Arthur Schopenhauer (1788-1860), a German philosopher known for his philosophy of pessimism, said that death *"is the truly inspiring genius of philosophy"*[2]. Maybe it is, especially when one considers that the inspiration for many a great work of art was a large, dose of depression.

I prefer not to summarily dismiss his fear that death will plunge one into a black abyss as all possibilities in thought should be considered. However, the evidence for survival of the soul is numerous, albeit, still yet to be scientifically proven.

The idea of immortality, resurrection, or the belief in life after death has existed in the human intellect since primitive times.

According to George E. Barker in his work, *Death and After Death*:

"Unless identity and continuity are both maintained, there is no real 'survival'. It was no doubt in this sense that Tennyson once wrote that if there were no immortality, he would hurl himself into the sea; or that Otto von Bismark declared that if he could not hope for an afterlife, this one would not be worth the effort of getting dressed in the morning; or that led Freud, for all his pathological treatment of it, to acknowledge that the belief that death is but the door to a bet-

5

ter life is 'the oldest, strongest, and most insistent wish' of humankind[3]."

Within recent years, the market has been flooded with books dealing with near death experiences. Some of these books have been written by those who have experienced near death, and some have been written by respected, well educated, medical professionals in varied fields of medical disciplines, who have collected data.

While doing research for this book, I was very surprised to find out where some of the first funding for this type of medical research originated.

The interesting case of James Kidd arose in 1964. Mr. Kidd was a miner in Phoenix, Arizona. He appeared to be poor, even borrowing tools for his mining expeditions and living in the cheapest room he could rent[4].

He left on a mining expedition 9 November 1949 and never returned. He was declared dead a few years later. When a safe-deposit box in a Douglas, Arizona bank was opened because the rent was long overdue, a large number of securities were found. A will, scribbled in pencil on a piece of paper, was also found. It read:

"this is my first and only will and is dated the second of January 1946. I have no heirs and have not been married in my life and after all my funeral expenses have been paid and $100. One hundred dollars to some preacher of the gospel to say farewell at my grave sell all my property which is all in cash and stocks with E.F. Hutton Co Phoenix some in safety deposit box, and have this balance money to go in a research or some scientific proof of a soul of the human body which leaves at death I think in time their (sic) can be a Photograph of soul leaving the human at death, James Kidd[5].

Little is known about James Kidd. He lived a very simple, reclusive life.

A fellow miner called him a "book-head[6]," saying:

"You could learn from Jim, because he always had something to offer. I used to tell the other boys, 'Stop, drink, and listen, fellows, and you'll learn.'" [7]

After a long litigation among 130 contenders, Kidd's $270,000 legacy was granted to the American Society of Psychical Research (ASPR)[8]. Its aim was to test the following hypothesis:

"We present the hypothesis that some part of the human personality indeed is capable of operating outside the living body (becoming ecsomatic) on rare occasions, and that it may continue to exist after the brain processes have ceased and the organism is decayed[9]."

Why did James Kidd think that the soul could be photographed as it left the body at death? Had he witnessed the phenomenon, but no photograph backed up his experience?

None will ever know the personal motivation behind James Kidd's bequest. Nevertheless, I would venture to say that some of those who I have interviewed over the last few years, who have experienced the supernatural, including myself, just might venture a good guess.

SUNRISE SUNSET

"I know I am deathless."
Walt Whitman
Leaves of Grass[10]

I did not wait for spring this year. I dreaded its coming; I resented its rude promise of nature's renewal as it flowed steadily, relentlessly, towards us. As though alive, it approached with purpose on a raging, river of time. Nothing could stop it. My husband and I were trapped in its violent current.

One was drowning. Two were drowning. Death disguised as time.

Now just he and I watched the sunrises together. He and I watched the sunsets. He and I relished each day; he and I talked of death.

I brought him home, away from the sterile, hollow, halls of the hospital where the air hung thick and heavy. He had been there for 8 days, as his condition steadily deteriorated. There was no medical hope for his survival; three days was about all they expected him to live. The attending cancer physician said there would be no follow-up appointments. She smiled sheepishly as she handed me a five-day prescription of useless antibiotics...no refills. It was a Wednesday, clear and cold. Home's familiar embrace was the thing for which he yearned. Relieved that his wish was fulfilled, I watched as a calm peace came over his countenance as the ambulance attendants rolled his litter into our house.

He was bedridden, weak, and gravely ill, yet we knew just how lucky we were as he tenderly traced the line of my brow, his slender fingers lingering in the hollow of my temple.

"Lucky", he said, and smiled broadly, his comforting dimple flashing as I smiled and deftly cleared my cheek of tears.

Lucky. We had always been lucky. He was a cosmopolitan city boy; I was a country girl. It was a May - December romance made in heaven.

The son of Jewish, Russian immigrants, Sam came into this world in a cold water flat on New York's Lower East Side on 6 October 1916. He was named after twin boys in the family, Samuel, and Solomon, who had died in adolescence in Russia. His arrival was at sundown, on a Friday evening, the start of the Jewish Sabbath; it was also the start of Yom Kippur.

A fine figure of a man, he stood a slender, six feet two inches tall, with a full head of dark hair. A handsome man, his presence was surrounded by an air of distinguished sophistication. A musician, composer, and music publisher by profession, he played bass, tuba, violin, and trumpet and was once considered one of the top ten bass players in the business. Well known as a jazz musician, he was also a respected classical musician, studying under Tibor Serly (an associate of Bala Bartok) and Zoltan Kodaly. Considered a fine tuba player, it was Sam's good friend, Hank Stern, who taught him how to play.

His career spanned over 60 years in the music industry. As a teenager, his career started in the New York night clubs such as the famous Door, Leon and Eddies, the

Figure 1 Sam Fiedel and his wife, Dorothy, stands on their front porch in Columbia, Pennsylvania. - December 1989.

Hickory House, La Conga Club, the Stork Club, and he worked as a regular musician on New York's Tin Pan Alley. At age 17, he joined the CBS staff orchestra, where he received what he considered his 'lucky break' playing CBS's *The Lucky Strike Hit Parade*. The musicians in the CBS band called him "the wonder boy", a name he always recalled with a little embarrassment and a chuckle.

A humble man, he seldom acknowledged his successful career was due solely to talent. He attributed much of his success to conductor Marc Warnow, the man he considered his mentor, and to good, old, 'lady' luck.

Descended from a long line of musicians, it seems that 'lady' luck, for the Fiedels, was always music...even in the old country.

Sam's grandfather, a Jewish rabbi in Russia, was also a musician. Due to his grandfather's great skill as a trumpet player, and great skill as a horseman, Grandfather Fiedel rode with and was a most unlikely member of the elite, royal guard of the Russian Cossacks[*].

Sam's rabbi/Cossack grandfather helped many people flee Russia. His son, Max Fiedel, Sam's father, who was born in Russia, was also a fine trumpet player. When it came time for him to flee the mother country, he tucked his trumpet under his worn coat lapel, let it protrude conspicuously, and posed as a musician-vagrant who slept in the gutters. It was this persona, as a "bum with a horn, tucked neatly in his coat along with lady luck" that enabled Sam's father to escape Russia, and flee across Europe. The people who Sam's grandfather had helped flee, in turn, helped Sam's father.

World War II interrupted Sam's professional career. Just weeks after graduating from New York University, he was drafted into the Army and shipped out to North Africa (Tunisia) to chase Rommel across the desert. A shrapnel wound sent him stateside just 9 days after his arrival in Africa. He recovered, played in the Army band for a short stint, and received an honorable discharge at

---

[*] It is very unusual that a Jew, least of all a rabbi, would be a Cossack. The elite cavalry guard, more accurately described as the Czar's henchmen, murdered, plundered and rode a rein of terror on the Russian, Jewish population by order of the Czar. The fact that Isaac Fiedel was a Jew was overlooked because of his talent as a trumpet player. Fiedel, however, was a double agent, and headed up a group called the "Schlagers" (the "Slayers"). This secret militia, in turn, reined terror on the Cossacks.

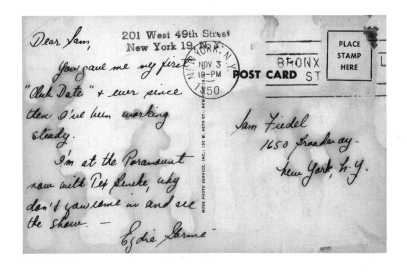

Figure 2 Sam touched the lives of many. This postcard dated Nov. 3, 1950 reads: "Dear Sam, You gave me my first 'club Date' & ever since then I've been working steady. I'm at the Paramount now with Tex Beneke, why don't you come in and see the show – Eydie Gorme "

war's end. He returned to CBS after the war as the "Golden Age" of radio and television continued to unfold. He went on to do such shows as *The Jackie Gleason Show, The Ed Sullivan Show, The Woolworth Hour with Percy Faith,* and *Arthur Godfrey's Talent Scouts.*

Imagine my surprise, when after our first date, Sam walked through the headlights of my car, tipped his hat at me, and actually put me into what might be called a state of mental shock.

It was weeks before I could explain my strange reaction to his innocent wave of goodbye. The explanation was also quite unusual.

When I was a little girl, I had a crush on two television personalities. Sid Caesar was one. The man in the band that Arthur Godfrey would introduce at the beginning of each show, was the other. I recall I sat on the floor and waited for Arthur Godfrey to introduce the man with the large violin, and I was thoroughly delighted when this man on the television would tip his imaginary hat at me. Each time I saw him, I would ask my grandmother whom he was. She usually hesitated and then said "Sammy", but I was not satisfied and would ask again. I finally realized Grandmother did not know the man, and she was not going to tell me anymore about him than Arthur Godfrey did.

I think it is very likely that I told her I was going to marry him; I liked him so much. I say this because I was also going to marry Sid Caesar, of course, that wedding would take place right after I married my daddy. Who would have guessed that fate would join two people, separated by age, time, geography, and culture, …such an unlikely match, 30 years down the road?

Sam's career was never boring. He worked with such entertainers as Dinah Shore, Frank Sinatra, Tony Bennet, Vic Damone, Peggy Lee, Jack Parr, Red Buttons, Danny Kaye, Jane Froman, Bob Hope, Henny Youngman, J. C. Flippin, Ricky Ricardo, Lucille Ball and Anne Miller.

He also worked with the Johnny Green Orchestra and the Myer Davis Orchestra playing debutante balls at the Waldorf-Astoria, and the Plaza Hotel in New York City. While playing a society job, one of Sam's acquaintances pulled him aside and asked if he would like to see the next president of the United States. The friend then pointed out the couple walking by; it was John Fitzgerald Kennedy with his then fiancée, Jackie. The society job was at the Hyannis Port Kennedy compound.

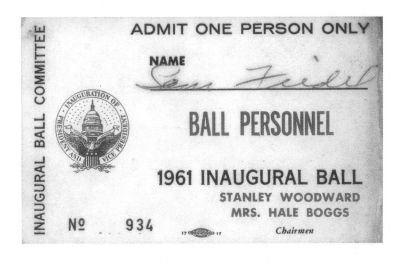

INAUGURAL BALL COMMITTEE

ADMIT ONE PERSON ONLY

NAME

BALL PERSONNEL

1961 INAUGURAL BALL
STANLEY WOODWARD
MRS. HALE BOGGS
Chairmen

N⁰ 934

Figure 3 John Kennedy was pointed out to Sam as being the next president of the United States several years before Kennedy ran for the office. A few years later Sam played in the orchestra at one of Kennedy's inaugural balls in Washington, DC. Above is Sam's entrance pass to the ball.

The friend certainly had the inside scoop. A few years later Sam played at one of Kennedy's inaugural balls in Washington, DC. Sam often said he never worked a day in his life; because to him, being a musician was just plain fun. He kept bass fiddles in a dozen studios all over New York City as he ran from one job to the next.

Sam also worked Broadway and played such shows as *Foxy*, *The Follies Bergère*, *George M* with Joel Gray, *Coco* with Katherine Hepburn, *Oklahoma* with Gordon MacRae, *My Fair Lady* with Rex Harrison, *Lorelei* with Carol Channing, *I Remember Mama* with Liv Ullmann, and *The King and I* with Yul Brynner, to name just a few.

Figure 4 Sam Fiedel (standing with bass) kept instruments in a dozen recording studios throughout New York City. He was photographed above, on a job. Note the recording equipment in foreground. Photo credit: David Workman, N.Y.C.

Rather jaded when it came to Broadway however, he insisted that every Broadway show was alike, *"...just half a tone higher."*

The "rat race" of New York City and the entertainment business, lost its luster as Sam approached retirement age.

"What for...what are they building?" he would ask, as many of his friends dropped dead chasing the next job. He recalled the incident in an orchestra pit where the lead trumpet player slumped over, lifeless in his chair.

The conductor was informed of the man's condition, but was more concerned that the orchestra would miss the opening cue.

The conductor then tapped his baton on his music stand and said to the dead man's shocked and bewildered, fellow musicians, *"See if you can get him to play just the opening fanfare!"*

Sobered, yet satisfied with his professional achievements, Sam would again repeat: *"What am I building? Am I ever going to write something better than Mozart, or Bach? I don't think so..."*

So, the tall, handsome bassist, who had dated some of the most beautiful, and some of the most wealthy, women in the world, yet managed to remain a bachelor, put down his bow and tuba and went on vacation.

He met and married me and often said his last 17 years were the happiest in his life. They were the best years of my life.

It was indeed a happy marriage. It was the kind few people ever have and the kind so many only dream about. Age, religion, time, and sickness did not separate us, for we were inseparable. We thoroughly enjoyed each other's company and were always together. And when Sam developed cancer, he didn't just have it. *We* had cancer.

We did not know how much longer we would be together. He requested that I put him in front of our window to the world, which I had arranged, even before he spoke his request. The new addition to our home had a twenty foot wall of windows which looked out over the Lancaster County countryside where we could watch eagles soar and storm clouds gather. As if by Divine intervention, all of the cloaks of the four seasons unfurled outside our wall of glass in those last 31 days of his life.

There was winter's coating of crystal that covered the trees and shimmered in the dawn's light. Then, snow came at night as fluffy, white down that softly floated to the ground turning our view of the world into a beautiful, serene, postcard. There were thunderstorms, horrific lightning, then bitter cold. Three seasons in a month, and I dreaded the coming of the fourth, the warm winds of spring.

On several occasions during that last month, I thought I would lose him. His mind was still sharp and he was very much aware of all that was going on around him. A few Tylenol was the extent of the medication he took for his discomfort, and he had refused the antibiotics that did nothing to improve his condition, but upset his stomach and made him feel worse.

His complexion could turn several colors of the spectrum in a few short minutes turning from chalky white, to yellow, green, and gray. One late afternoon, the first occasion that I thought I might lose him, I watched helplessly as his breathing became more rapid and labored his pulse weak and rapid. I knew he was dying and frantically I called Hospice, knowing that my telephone call was more for me than it was for him. It was my desperate way of seeking to stop the inevitable.

My distressed telephone call then set off a flurry of telephone interruptions by the well meaning Hospice. Each inquiry, less informed than the last, asked me how he was doing. By the forth or fifth call, I said that he seemed a bit better, and that I thought that the crisis had passed. The caller insisted that I "chat" with her because I, that's right, I *"didn't sound very good"*.

" Lady, my husband is dying…how am I supposed to sound?" I snapped back, after I had scurried out of my husband's earshot, tears flowing from a bucket, which was always full.

The last thing I needed was a psychological evaluation of my mental state. I told her I appreciated the concern, but if nothing could be done for my husband, please don't waste my valuable time by forcing me to give patient case updates to uninformed, though, well meaning, Hospice employees. Each call forced me to leave my dying husband's side. It was then that I decided, when that final moment came it would be, as it should be, between us.

That time came again shortly before sunrise a couple of weeks later. It was just before dawn on a Sunday morning after he had drunk a cup of tea and eaten a small cookie, that I watched him as he started to fade. He was pasty white, his pulse weak and extremely rapid and intermittent but he continued to talk to me about our sad predicament and his fast approaching death.

We both agreed that I would not awaken our son and daughter-in-law who slept soundly in the upstairs' bedroom, for if death would come, it would greet just the two of us. The sun rose as I held his hand, my head resting on the arm of the chair, close to his body. Sam had weakened; each breath labored, his eyes closed against the new dawn.

Then suddenly, he opened his eyes. His gaze fixed on an object located behind me. I watched his eyes follow that, which I did not see. With a most curious look on his face, and lifting his head off of its cushion, Sam's gaze followed whatever it was, pass in front of his chair, and out the wall of windows situated to the front and left of him. Exhausted, his head fell back in the chair, his eyes closed once more.

"Honey," he said the next moment, as he again opened his weary eyes, *"don't worry...I'll be alright...but*

only for a little while...they didn't speak, but they decided to give us a little more time..."

Indeed, his pulse was stronger, more regular, his coloring was better; it was a decided change from a few moments earlier. He then described the two dark, cloaked and hooded figures, which he saw walk behind me and in front of him. He said that where the faces should have been in the hood openings, there was black emptiness and so he could place no facial identity to the figures although he knew that they were Death.

He said he did not know if he was hallucinating, but the figures walked behind me, and paused in front of him, both looking at the two of us. The cloaked ones then nodded their heads at Sam and turned and floated past us, passing through the elevated foot of his chair, through portions of a table situated at the window, and passed through the slightly opened windows, out into the yard, and disappeared.

Sam remarked with wonder and repeated their purpose, *"They passed right through the windows...I don't think I was just seeing things... They have given me a short reprieve...I'll be alright, but just for a little while though..."*

Sure enough, Sam rallied; I made him another cup of tea, and coaxed a few morsels of food into him, as I thanked God for giving us ...just a little more time.

Was my husband hallucinating as he watched the cloaked and hooded figures nod a reprieve? I do not think so, but whether it was a hallucination or not, the result was as indicated; he did get better for a short time.

During Sam's 31 days at home, he had few complaints. He was more worried about me, than he was about himself and voiced his concerns to a little 'angel' named Jessie Drey who, to me, worked disguised as a registered nurse. She worked for Hospice of Lancaster County and would stop by three times a week too access Sam's condition and suggest ways to help make him more comfortable during his illness.

Sam had been home about 12 days, and he started to complain that I (his wife) never slept. I had moved a bed into our windowed world and slept about 10 feet away from his side. He needed round the clock care, and I seldom left the room for more than 5 minutes at a time. Although the sleep I got could be counted more in intervals of minutes during the day and night; I indeed did sleep enough to keep me alert and able to function without much distress.

Sam, however, worried about me constantly. With tears welling up in his eyes, a very uncommon emotional condition for Sam, he would tell Jessie: *"My God, she never sleeps...never...all I have to do is just look at her and her head pops up off the pillow...day or night, day or night...she never sleeps...I'm killing her...my God I'm killing her..."*

I tried to tell him that he was wrong. I was sleeping.

"How could I look so good if I was not sleeping?" I asked, as I winked and posed model- style.

As the three of us laughed, I assured Jessie Angel that although I did get up many times a night; I was sleeping enough.

Sam's protests continued. He anguished over my health and mentioned his concern each time Jessie Angel visited. It was only about seven or 8 days later that I realized that it was not Sam's imagination that when he looked at me, I got up. The revelation hit me one early morning as I made my way to his side in the firelight and asked him if he called me.

"No, but I thought about calling you though..." he said.

Sam did not imagine that my head popped up when he looked at me. Because, much to both of our surprise, not once during the entire time that he had been home had he verbally, called my name aloud for assistance. All he had to do was just *think* that he needed me and I awoke from the depths of slumber. Knowing this helped to ease his anxiety.

During Sam's last days he rallied and retreated several times, each retreat leaving him weaker than the last. The last two weeks of his life, he became increasingly agitated as sunset approached for he feared he would not live to see the sun rise again.

I felt helpless, because I would do anything for him but it was beyond my power to stop the sun from setting.

THURSDAY, MARCH 26, 1998 – 1 AM

The lack of sleep had started to catch up with me, as Sam became increasingly restless and agitated with the onset of nightfall. My sleep periods had become shorter and shorter in the last 5 days, and physically I was about to collapse. Our son, Justin, who was on emergency leave from the Navy, pulled the night shift that night allowing me to get about 3 hours of sleep. I awoke refreshed two hours before dawn to find Sam somewhat better and relieved we could watch another sunrise together.

He spent a lot of time talking about our sons and how much he loved them and told me about his new discovery. Sam was very happy Justin had stayed up the night with him and had discovered something about Justin that he had not noticed before.

"Justin is an angel and guess what...he is just like you...I never realized just how much like you he is. He thinks like you, feels (emotionally) like you...he is just like you...just like you...and I never realized it," he said.

That day, the doctor prescribed some anti-anxiety medicine hoping to calm him with his fear of sunset. Although the doctor had prescribed morphine for Sam when he was brought home from the hospital, Sam refused to take it for fear he would become a drug addict[*]. He finally agreed to have the morphine in the house after the nurse convinced him it could help his labored and rapid respiration.

THURSDAY, MARCH 26, 1998–AFTER SUNSET

The anti-anxiety medicine was working. Though he was still upset with the coming of nightfall, he was more relaxed. He had stopped eating about four days prior and I was happy if I could coax a small bite of cracker or a few sips of watermelon juice into him. He dozed in and out of fitful sleep, talking and mumbling to unseen visitors.

He remarked that the room was very crowded with people when he slept, but he did not know who they were.

---

[*] Sam was the consummate professional musician. He had watched many men, some gifted geniuses in the music business, ruin their marriages, families, and careers from drug use. Sam did not use drugs or alcohol and did not intend to start this late in life.

After midnight however, he did not want to sleep; so, we talked through the wee hours of the morning.

We talked about how lucky we were to have this time together for so many never get the opportunity to say goodbye. For us there were no "I'm sorry's" for we never had a marriage like that.

His only regret was that we were not married sooner and that he did not want to leave me. He had never cried in his life until now, but said his tears were not for himself. He said he was crying for the world, for the starving, for the homeless, and wondered how can man treat man so callously.

He told me what he wanted to wear for his burial; and instructed me how to arrange his body immediately after his death.

After drifting into sleep for a few moments, he awoke and out of the clear blue sky inquired about an old friend from New York named Henry.

"Do you think Henry is gone?" he asked.

I replied, *"Do you mean dead... Oh, I am sure we would have been contacted if something happened to him. Do you want me to try and contact him?"*

Sam replied that it was no use and he thought that maybe Henry had passed away. The subject of Henry was never discussed again.

As the morning crept toward the dawn, Sam and I talked about death. Sam's analogy for death was that he was dressed and ready to travel. His said that his bags were packed and he was standing in the train station with the tickets in his out stretched hand, but nobody was there to take his ticket.

FRIDAY, MARCH 27, 1998 – 7 AM

Sam was worse than I had ever seen him; he was choking, unable to breathe as the fluid in his lungs from the pneumonia smothered him. He had ripped the oxygen tubes from his nose earlier in the morning. He said the noise was deafening, the oxygen didn't help him breathe and he could stand it no longer.

I knew he needed more than the three drops of morphine he permitted me to give him earlier that morning. I needed help for him now, for I did not feel qualified to administer the dosage I thought he might require. It was then that I went against the decision not to call Hospice when Sam's time was close. Sam needed help; I called Jessie Angel.

Arrangements were made to have a full-time nurse at the house around the clock. The morphine dosage was increased and within an hour and a half Sam had slipped into a paralyzed state, unable to talk or move, each breath labored and shallow. It was Friday morning, March 27, 1998. He was dying.

Rabbi Shaya Sackett, an Orthodox rabbi came to our home. Although he had never met Sam or me, I sensed a warm aura of compassion surrounding him. Sam was a devout Jew who practiced his faith. He was fluent in Hebrew and although he belonged to a synagogue in New York City, he insisted that his temple was anywhere that he prayed. The differences in our religion never posed a problem for us; our love, respect and devotion transcended even those differences, but I was still a bit apprehensive that it might pose a problem for an Orthodox rabbi.

Rabbi Sackett assured me there was no problem. He left with me a Hebrew prayer book.

25

Spring had come that day, almost as an omen; it arrived the day he was to die. The air was warm and a gentle breeze blew. The temperature was about 78 degrees; the sun was hot. As Sam had requested earlier in the morning, every window and door in the large windowed room was opened, and the ceiling fan of the room was on 'high' circulating in a downward direction. I had placed a 25-inch floor fan beside Sam's chair, as he had wanted, for he said he felt he was suffocating and the breeze helped to ease his suffering.

The full-time nurse could not tell me how long Sam had to live. It could be hours or even days. For death, as does birth, comes in its own time. She did tell me that she would inform me when she saw changes that indicated the time was close and repeated the phrase she would use, to me twice.

There were seven in attendance with my husband who included our two sons, our daughter- in- law, my sister, a friend, the nurse, and me. Evening was approaching and his condition remained unchanged, unable to talk or respond, each breath labored and shallow.

I felt helpless, what could I do for him? I left his side for a moment and as I sat in the evening sun on the back porch, I read the Hebrew prayer book that the rabbi had left with me. As I read one particular prayer, it struck me that it was a prayer meant for Sam. I knew Sam almost as well as I knew myself, and I felt the words I read addressed some of the fears and unresolved anxieties that life had left etched on his heart. I felt compelled to pray it for him, in sincere hope that God would answer.

I rushed to his side and sat close, my head leaning close to his ear as I prayed the prayer out loud. Within 15 seconds after completing the prayer, I heard a voice intruding into our world, *"Dottie...Dottie..."*

As I reluctantly relinquished my mental seclusion, I realized that it was the nurse trying to get my attention. I heard her say the phrase she promised she would say when she saw the end approaching.

"Dottie," she said, *"I see changes..."*

I looked at her with an incredulous stare. I did not want to leave his side but it was instinct that caused me to jump to my feet. I raced to the living room to seek out one of Sam's prayer books for another prayer to read for him. As I frantically shuffled through the pages, some unseen force stopped me mid shuffle. At that moment, I realized that Sam was going to leave without me and I should immediately return to his side.

I raced back into the room, and watched as things transpired in slow motion. Our friend Mary, and the nurse, was beside Sam. Mary had placed her hand on Sam's arm and held the nurse's hand with the other. The nurse had her free hand raised upward as Mary recited the rosary.

They noticed my arrival and slowly parted to allow me to take my place at the side of my husband. Sam's breathing was unchanged. As I held his hand, and told him I was there, he took several more breaths, and then...

There were none. Quiet, peaceful. There was utter silence. No sound, as if the world had paused in respect.

I sat motionless and numb. I had prayed for the healing, that Sam was to be the victor in the struggle of life and death, and now I knew not which he was.

I recall hearing the Hospice nurse remark: *"That was beautiful, just beautiful..."*

As I gazed at his motionless face, I blinked my eyes several times. I was sure that the faint, luminous glow surrounding his mouth and nostrils was an illusion. Curiously, each time I opened my eyes, the white glow remained, as it appeared to increase in density.

The nurse was moving, as if in a dream around his body, checking for signs of life. She then returned to her seat situated about 6 feet away and began writing. She returned a second time, in what I would guess was a few minutes later, again feeling for a pulse. She walked around his body, from ankles, to groin, and then behind him to feel the carotid artery in his neck.

It was about this time that the soft luminous glow I had seen hovering around his mouth and nose, changed. Much to my amazement, a white, luminous, smoke started to curl out of Sam's mouth. A little smoke at first, steadily increasing in volume. I blinked, but realized that I indeed was not seeing things and inquired of the nurse now sitting close by, *"What is the smoke coming out of Sam's mouth?"*

She looked at me calmly, a vaguely, curious expression on her face, as I repeated the question. She shook her head to the negative, then shrugged her shoulders, and went back to her paperwork.

The volume of smoke was now increasing, tendrils began to exit his mouth and both nostrils. It was at this moment that I was almost over come with a feeling of awe.

"Ahhhhhh…" I felt the sound, soft, and full, uncontrollably roll out of my mouth, as some basal, primeval, part of my soul realized just what I was seeing. Sam was letting me see his soul, we do have a soul, and it was real, it had shape, it had form.

"Ohhhh…" I thought, *"…what a wonderful gift…Sam's soul…and I'm being permitted to see it…"*

The thought flashed through my mind that maybe I could touch it, embrace it, but just as quickly as the thought came, I knew the answer. I should not touch it for it would be a sacrilege, to do so would violate my husband's very essence. My touch would dirty that which was so pure.

The smoke now rose thick and fast, in luminous, curling, tendrils that danced several inches above his face. I asked again, my question meant for the nurse, my question meant for the whole room. What was the smoke? Again the nurse shrugged her shoulders and not a sound came from anyone in the room.

"Do you see the smoke?" I rephrased my question. Again, I received no reply.

I watched in amazement as it curled and twisted, thick and dense and began to collect into an elliptical ball about 8 inches above his face. It was in the shape of a small football about 6 inches in length, the ends rounded, and it increased in density as it was being fed by the ethereal mist of life.

My moment of awe was interrupted by the nurse who said, *"Dottie, time of death 5:40 PM."* I nodded in acknowledgement.

It was then that I realized why the nurse did not answer my question about the smoke. It was because she did not see it. I again asked if anyone saw the smoke as our youngest son, Justin, came into the room and stood at Sam's head.

"Yes, I see it Mom…" was his quiet, solemn, and matter-of-fact reply.

I think I might have felt a bit relieved at his answer, for I could not understand why no one else could see it. It was white and starkly contrasted against a dark, burgundy chair.

The round shape continued to hover over his face, as the amount of smoke feeding the form lessened. It remained stationary in the air, unaffected by the surrounding environment. It did not dissipate; it did not float away. It was as if it was there, and then, suddenly, it was not there.

I do not know how long this event lasted. Time stood still. A guess for me would be about 10 minutes; but I do not think I will ever know for sure.

AFTER SAM. MY INQUIRY...

After Sam's death, I spoke to the rabbi and told him of my experience. I thought that perhaps he could shed some insight or clarity on the event and wondered if, theologically, he had a problem with my experience.

The rabbi told me that as a rabbi, he had no problem with my belief that I saw Sam's soul as it exited his body.

I then spoke at length to our family doctor, about the unusual occurrence.

Being the true, analytical, scientist I know the doctor is, we discussed everything that could have possibly influenced the event I witnessed. The doctor thought that there had to be a scientific explanation although he had never read about any similar phenomena recorded at the time of death. We discussed every possible explanation, from the physiological conditions of Sam's body, environmental temperature and air currents, to condensation and evaporation. No feasible, scientific answer was deduced.

It is interesting to note, that the smoke and cloud that formed was totally unaffected by the large, 36" ceiling fan that was on 'high' blowing the air in a downward direction in the room, almost directly above the patient's head. It was also unaffected by the floor fan situated approximately 4 feet to the left and front of Sam, and turned on 'high'. Room temperature was about 80 degrees, which would have eliminated a cloud formed by condensation.

Our doctor concluded it must have been an "other worldly" occurrence since all other scientific possibilities were ruled out. Although it is possible that the doctor's conclusion was influenced by a widow's grief, our discussion was scientifically oriented.

I searched the libraries looking for similar records of this kind of occurrence. Most references were studies of near-death experiences (NDE's); recounted by ones *not brought back from the dead*, but from ones rescued from a point *very close to death*. There were few accounts of unusual events witnessed by those who attended the death of another. However, this interesting account from around the turn of the century, appeared in the *Encyclopaedia of Psychic Science:*

> *"Watchers by the death-bed often hear rushing sounds and see some kind of curious luminosity. Dr. H. Baraduc attempted to secure photographic record when his son and wife died. He found that in each case a luminous, cloud-like mass appeared over the bodies and impressed the photographic plate[11]."*

There was something about my experience that bothered me; it was many weeks before I made a connection. I happen to know a gentleman who claims to take photographs of ghosts. Rick Fisher's photographic hobby has been covered in some of Lancaster, Pennsylvania's local newspapers with a velvet gloved, editorial hand that at times tweaks of subtle ridicule. His photos capture what he calls spirit energy in the form of "orbs", "ectoplasm" and "vortexes". Rick many times uses two different cameras, one digital, and one regular 35 mm, to take the same shot. The images show up on both sets of prints and negatives.

I finally made the comparative connection. This "ectoplasm" resembling smoke, which has also shown up in photographs of certain sites located on the Gettysburg, Pennsylvania battlefield, very closely resembles what I witnessed curling out of my husband's mouth and nose. Interesting.

Is it possible that the energy, which escapes our body at the time of death, is out of phase with the energy that oscillates in this reality? Are the anomalies that Rick Fisher captures on film actually what he suggests that they are…spirit energy of the deceased? Maybe.

I remember one of the last things Sam said to me about our son, Justin: *"…he's just like you"*.

Indeed, ultimately, only Justin and I saw the luminous smoke. We compared notes about six weeks after the event. Justin described the exact same thing that I saw.

It is interesting to note here, that the appearance of cloaked and hooded figures to the dying is not an unusual, or unrecorded phenomena. Karlis Osis, Ph.D. and Erlendur Haraldsson, Ph.D., in their book, At *The Hour Of Death*, recorded paranormal experiences in just this form, while doing hundreds of studies of cases, both Hindus and Christians, Indians and Americans, to collect data to determine the subjective experiences the patients had at the portal of death[12].

After a recent speaking engagement, a woman asked me if Sam had had any prophetic information. She explained that she worked as a Hospice nurse for 6 years and several times the dying patient knew something that he should not have known.

Aristotle wrote in his treatise on *Sleeping and Waking*,

> *"...that the terminally ill, whose sensory powers have declined, are able to peer into the future due to the strengthening of their imagination. The latter organ is no longer distracted by the interference of the sensory powers. Much of this can also be found in the Talmud, viz., that statements made on the deathbed are given credence as if they were prophetic[13]."*

A day after Sam's death, I tried in vain to contact his friend Henry from New York City. Sadly, I learned that Henry had passed away... a year ago.

Sam related to me that he was told as a child, his hour of birth, a Friday evening at sundown, the start of the Sabbath, and the first day of Yom Kippur, was considered a special time to be born. It is interesting to note that Sam's dread of the approaching sunset was not unfounded.

Ultimately, he died as he was born, on a Friday, at sunset, at the start of the Sabbath. The rabbi verified that that time of day according to the Hebrew faith, is considered an honorable, chosen time, for birth and death.

I read over the prayers that I prayed for Sam on that fateful day. The last of which was a "Special Tehillim for the Sick".

I had not noticed, on the day of Sam's death, the special description accompanying the prayer.

Written in Italics and small print it read: *"This is an excellent prayer for any person who is sick or in distress. Anyone who offers this prayer with heartfelt devotion is assured that God will accept it[14]."*

I know that what I witnessed the day of my husband's death was Sam's very essence, his soul. I feel grateful, that I was given the special gift of a vision that transcended the need for faith. Grateful that we had those special days together; and honored that I was chosen as his wife.

I hope my story helps to ease the sorrow, the grief, or the emptiness of just one person who has lost a loved one, who finds their conviction of faith, has frailties and has wavered. Let me assure them that there is more to us than flesh and bone, and that which is truly important, never dies.

As for me, I will never watch another sunrise or sunset without sharing it with my Sam as I contemplate a thought that contradicts our reality.

There is a point the sun reaches, as it hangs above the horizon, which defies the senses. At that special moment, when the East, West, North, and South are unknown, even the most skilled sailor could not determine if he was gazing upon a rising or a setting sun.

Is it the beginning or the end of the day? Is it the alpha or the omega, which unfolds in all its heavenly glory? The answer is quite simple.

It is both...

THE ACCOMAC INN
GHOST

*"Oh youth or young man, ... in every succession of life and
death you will do and suffer what like may fitly suffer at the hands of
like..."*

Plato[15]

The road that leads to the Accomac Inn winds through the countryside of York County, Pennsylvania like a serpent. It emerges from the wooded hills along the riverbank of the Susquehanna River where the beholder's eye is greeted with a wide, flat, watery, expanse of uneventful landscape.

One might wish that Mother Nature had introduced a protruding rock or two, an island, or a shoreline cliff, to break up the broad expanse of water. Nevertheless, it is this lack of intrusion where in its beauty lay. Peaceful and serene, an occasional call of a wild bird echoes through the air.

The limestone, Accomac Inn stands solid and stately, boldly facing the placid river. One can not help but notice her, for she appears massive and well kept, a staircase of stone leading to her door. As with many old, historical structures, there have been reports that the Inn is haunted.

The tract of land on which the Accomac Inn was built has the distinction of being the first official land grant on the west bank of the Susquehanna River. The first sur

Figure 5 The Accomac Inn burned in 1935. It was rebuilt shortly thereafter and is believed to mirror the structure first opened as a tavern and inn in 1775.

-vey for the 200 acre tract of land called "The Partner's Adventure", was completed in 1722 for Philip Syng and Thomas Brown by the state of Maryland. This particular grant was the most northern grant made by Maryland in what would later become Pennsylvania territory[16].

Twenty years later, partner, Philip Syng, sold his land to James Anderson, who began to operate a ferry from the east shore of the river – now Marietta, Lancaster County. Anderson Ferry received its official charter on November 17, 1742[17]. Apparently, people had been crossing the river at this point from as early as 1725[18].

No one knows exactly when the Accomac was erected, but records indicate that "...by 1775, Anderson's Ferry Inn had been built", and by 1800 it had secured a Tavern license from the York County Courts[19].

Many distinguished American Revolutionaries crossed the river at this point during Colonial times, as the road to Accomac was at one time the main artery of travel from the New England States, and New York.

One of the most notable visitors of the Inn was the Marquis de Lafayette. The Marquis was a good friend of George Washington, the father of our country. It could be said that Lafayett was the equivalent of the fair-haired boy who becomes the boss's right-hand man in business today. The Father of our country met the Marquis at a dinner on July 31, 1777 in Philadelphia. Washington was so drawn to the smiling 19 -year -old nobleman, that he immediately invited him to join his inner circle. The Marquis was one of the few foreign military adventurers who was a credit to his profession. He was invaluable on the trip to Newport, with his command of the French language. From all reports, General Washington sat silently at these conferences, looking from face to face.[20]

Lafayette was described as being: *"about six feet tall...His face was oval with light, large and prominent eyes, a high forehead and aquiline nose. He did not possess what is commonly termed genius, nor was he a man of remarkable intellectual powers"* but he did possess strong integrity and General Washington was his model[21].

About one year after he met the General, Lafayette found himself in York (at that time, known as York town) conferring with Congress.

Two letters from the Marquis de Lafayett serve as evidence he stopped at Accomac. He wrote two notes to the honorable Henry Laurens (President of the Continental Congress) on February 3, 1778: from *"Anderson Ferry at three o'clock in a great hurry..."* and later that day,

Figure 6 The Marquis de Lafayette stopped at the Accomac Inn on February 3, 1778 on his way to Valley Forge and "...the river was full of ice". Photo: courtesy of the Historical Society of York, Pa.

crossed the Susquehanna at Anderson's Ferry...the river was full of ice[22]."

Some may venture a guess and say the Marquis de Lafayette roams the halls of the historic tavern. Much like the Hollywood depiction of Count Dracula who lined his coffin with home town Transylvanian dirt for his trip to America to ensure he got enough rest between bites,

Lafayette so loved his adopted country, that he had Virginia soil from the Colonies shipped to France to fill his own grave. Lafayette's body might have been in France, but he left his heart in Ol' Virginee. One might guess, if his final slumber were restless, geographic wise, America is the place he might choose to haunt.

However, no, the suspected ghosts of the Accomac Inn are a far more tragic type dating about a century later than the Marquis.

My visits have, of course, been more recent and the latest visit was under rather unusual circumstances. As I have informed my readers several times over the last few years, I do not investigate haunted places, I merely write about them. However, this day I was there on an investigation, as a curious observer.

I met Rick Fisher of Lancaster, Pa., (see pages 31 and 32) and Joan Barr of Dillsburg, Pa., at the Accomac Inn two days after the 1998 Thanksgiving holiday for a ghost investigation and photographing session. As a hobby, Rick and Joan investigate places suspected of being haunted and take photographs in hopes of capturing "spirit" energy on film.

Rick and Joan came armed with a Minolta Maxim 350 35-mm camera, a Sony Mavica, digital camera, a second digital camera, a video camera, an electromagnetic field sensing device and thermal scanners.

I came armed with a pen and paper and a 35-mm camera, which I found out later, did not work and has not, ever since.

Daniel L. MacDougall, a distinguished gentleman, who is the innkeeper and manager of the Accomac, greeted us cordially and gave us access to every room at the Inn, from attic to cellar. He filled us in on the history of the Inn, saying the original tavern and inn was destroyed in a fire in 1935 and the current building, built on the original foundation, is supposed to be very similar in appearance to that structure.

Curious if he had experienced any unusual or unexplained activity, I asked. He paused, smiled and said, *"No...but we did have a phantom diner in here recently..."*

Phantom diner? I thought. Could this mean disappearing mousse, or levitated silverware?

Mr. MacDougall then explained that the Phantom Diner reviews restaurants for a magazine called *Central Pa*. Working incognito, probably as a dining customer, the Phantom rates the restaurants he visits and publishes the results.

The Phantom described the restaurant's French cuisine in *Central PA's* October 1998 issue by saying, *"The food and service inside are each superb and have been so for at least 11 years...It may be the best all-around dining in the area[23]."*

The reported incidents of unusual occurrences at the Inn are probably less subtle than the Phantom Diner. According to Mr. MacDougall, guests, as well as restaurant staff, have had a few strange experiences.

It seems as if most of the activity takes place on the second floor of the Inn. The upstairs dining areas were, at one time, guestrooms for weary travelers. One particular incident involved Georgianne, one of the waitress staff. As she was rolling a serving cart out of the staff serving area along the hallway, she was quite startled to hear the high pitched chatting of a woman coming from the stairway area. She was startled because there were no customers in the restaurant at the time and she was working alone. She looked to find the source of the voice, but found no one or nothing to explain what she had just heard.

Sunday Brunch seems to be an active time for the unexplained. According to Mr. MacDougall, no less than three separate diners have reported they felt a strange presence in the upstairs ladies' restroom. Whether the guests were making a complaint or just a friendly informative observation to restaurant personnel, I can not say.

I do wonder how management, in an attempt at an explanation, would tactfully say: *"Well, it's probably just the ghost of a guy that was hanged and buried in the back yard...or his victim."*

Daniel MacDougall mentioned that a psychic had visited the restaurant a few years back, and kept getting the name: Doyle. It is interesting that the name is very similar to the real player in the horrible tragedy that took place at the Accomac in 1881.

From July 5, 1864 to 1899, the crossing and the Inn was known as "Coyle's Ferry". On May 30, 1881, John Coyle, Jr., son of the owner, shot and killed Emma Myers, an employee of the Coyle family. Johnny Coyle then turned the gun on himself, but was only superficially wounded, and survived the suicide attempt.

Emma Myers, the victim, was originally from Chambersburg, Pa, and was orphaned at age five. She lived in Marietta but stayed with the Coyle family to help Mrs. Coyle, who suffered from rheumatism. Emma was described as being very handsome, large of stature, but well proportioned, with a fair complexion, black hair, and large gray eyes. Although she was industrious and willing to work, she was said to be quite ignorant[24].

Garry Lehman in his article *Murder at Coyle's Ferry* wrote:

"That fateful morning, Emma was in the barn milking the cows. The parents of Johnny Coyle were asleep and John entered the barn with a loaded revolver and demanded that Emma marry him. She refused and Johnny shot her in the chest. Dr. M.J. McKennon of York did a post-mortem on the deceased, which revealed that the bullet passed through the middle of the sternum, five inches from the top. Ironically, the heart was directly under the sternum instead of inclining to the right as usual. If the heart had occupied its normal position, the bullet would have missed the heart and while the wound might have caused death, it would not have been immediately as in this case[25].

The defense based its case on insanity...John's mother and other witnesses testified to his (Coyle's) weakened mind from boyhood, his foolish and childish actions, conversation, and his general mental illness[26]."

Johnny Coyle was tried and convicted of first-degree murder. His first conviction was overturned and he was granted a new trial, with a change in venue. The new trial was held in Gettysburg, Adams County, Pa.; where he was again convicted and sentenced to death by hanging, nearly four years after the murder of young, Emma Myers.

The following are excerpts from the account of John Coyle's hanging as it appeared in the *York Gazette* of Tuesday, April 29, 1884 edition:

"On Tuesday morning last, at 11:25, John Coyle Jr. paid the penalty of his crime of mur-

dering Emily Myers, at his parents home, in Hellam Township, this county (York) on the 30th day of May 1881, on the gallows, in Gettysburg.

For several days before the execution, the town of Gettysburg was all-agog with excitement, and the opinion prevailed with many that he would yet cheat the gallows. Monday afternoon...medical experts of Philadelphia arrived and made an examination of Coyle's mental condition pronouncing him insane...but all to no avail, and a message was received about midnight saying 'The Governor would not interfere and Coyle must hang—sane or insane.'"

According to the *York Gazette*, the young Johnny Coyle was on an emotional roller coaster but regained his composure a day and a half before his execution.

On Monday morning, April 21, 1884, he asked his warden for some wine saying: *"I've never been any trouble to you, and I'll stand this bravely to the end. I only ask for wine for fear I may break down."*

The kindhearted warden gave him about a gill of wine.

Tuesday morning, April 22, 1884, Johnny awoke at 4 AM, and said he felt *"...first-rate"*. He then ate a hearty breakfast of Susquehanna shad beefsteak, coffee, bread, and butter.

The scaffold was erected in the rear portion of the jail yard with the execution set for 11 AM, but long before that, crowds started to congregate in and about the jail. Sheriff Plank issued about 340 ticket of admission, and none were to be admitted without the ticket. Several thousand people were present outside the jail and "scalpers" charged a premium as high as $5 (dollars) for one of the admission tickets[27].

As Johnny's hour of death approached, he sent for the Sheriff and requested that he *"do not let so many people into the hanging[28]."*

The York Gazette continues:

"At 10:30 (AM) the aged parents took their final leave of their son. The scene was a sad and affecting one, the old gray heads bowed over his shoulders, embracing him as only parents can embrace a child, the hot tears of deep grief and distress rolling fast and thick down over their wrinkled cheeks[29]."

According to the account, after the convicted man climbed the gallows, Johnny Coyle *"stood solid as a post, scarcely a muscle could be seen to move".*

The death warrant was read and the rope that was to spring the trap passed into the jail building, and by a hidden hand, was drawn at 11:25 AM. The platform dropped with a dull and heavy thud and the soul of John Coyle, Jr. was sent to meet its God[30].

According to the York Gazette, it took 20 minutes for Johnny to die. His body was cut down, then viewed by the jury, and then given over to friends of his family.

Johnny Coyle's body was taken home to the Accomac, late the same day, and buried beneath an apple tree on his father's farm not far from where he committed the terrible crime that cost him his life.

PHOTOGRAPHIC INVESTIGATION RESULTS

Forty minutes into the ghost photographic investigation, Joan Barr watched the screen of her digital camera as she held the magnetic field detector (EMF meter) while in the upstairs dining area (the Anderson Room) of the Accomac Inn. She observed the field detector register in the 2.5 to 7 milli gauss range, indicating an anomalous magnetic field increase. Simultaneously, the image screen of her digital camera became hazy.

Rick Fisher, who was also in the room at the time of the positive EMF meter reading, quickly snapped a digital picture. Rick explained:

> *"(One) must understand the anomaly would have had to pass through the detector for it to signal. I quickly took a photograph (when Joan signaled she had a reading) and captured an orb on the door beside her, the next set of photos taken after that resulted in nothing. They are very fast moving and each photograph is different."*

An attic scan was also productive. A bright orb was captured by digital camera among the roof rafters, and the possibility of the light being from a reflective source was ruled out.

According to Mr. Fisher, they obtained four digital pictures containing orbs, and twenty-five pictures using regular film yielded negative results.

Are these orbs evidence of spirit activity? Rick has had photographs from other investigations analyzed by a variety of experts. One opinion, from the digital camera manufacturer, stated that the orb was a pixel problem, but the company had no explanation for its occurrence. However, another picture, taken of the same anomaly with regular film, resulted in the orb captured on that photograph also. The orb was clearly defined on the negative.

Figure 7 This photograph of an orb (upper right center) was captured by digital camera in the attic of the Accomac Inn. Usually an electromagnetic field registering between 2.5 and 7.0 milli gauss is detected when this type of anomaly shows up on film. Photo courtesy of Rick Fisher.

How does one explain a digital image and a film emulsion producing the same results? Pixel problem?

Joan Barr commented that most of the incidents detected at the inn occurred in the Anderson Room. According to her, *"...this happened quite a few times."*

She finds this strange because the innkeeper said that they usually do not seat people in that room. Joan then commented that Daniel MacDougall (innkeeper) seemed almost surprised that this particular room recorded the most anomalous activity.

Has the victim of Johnny's affection found no peace? Does Emma Myers, who was so young and beautiful, yet so naïve, still innocently giggle at the approach of her admirer, still unaware the game is over? Is the ghost of the executed Johnny Coyle still roaming the space Johnny once called home? Does he remember the thud of the floor of the gallows as it opened into eternity so many years ago?

Johnny's mother claimed her son's body and transported it by wagon to their home at Accomac. He is buried about 50 feet south of the Inn in a grave marked with a stone which simply reads:

My Son

John D. Coyle

Born

March 15, 1855

Died

April 22, 1884

Aged 29 years, 1 month and 7 days

"Mother dear,

weep not for I am not dead

but sleeping here."

Possibly, there is more truth in that simple inscription than most realize.

ROUTINE CALL

"I very much doubt if anyone has the faintest idea of what is meant by the reality of anything but our own egos."

Arthur Eddington (1882-1944)

S everal years ago I had the opportunity to interview a police officer who worked on a police force in one of Lancaster County, Pennsylvania's municipalities. At his request, I will not reveal his real name or place of employment, but will call him Officer Smith.

Officer Smith was a young man in his early 30's, in good physical shape and clearly intellectually suited for the great responsibility an officer of the law, by necessity, shoulders. He proceeded to tell my husband and I about a very unusual thing that happened to him while on a call to a local home.

It was about 11 PM, one summer's night when neighbors who noticed lights in the house located next door to them, called the local police department. The house, though still containing furniture and personal property, had been closed up for several months, and the watchful neighbors thought that maybe a burglary was in progress.

The neighbor noticed a car in the driveway; but knew not to whom it belonged. The kitchen, which should have been dark, was now illuminated with light.

Officer Smith explained that he and his partner cautiously surveyed the situation, as there was indeed someone in the house. His partner checked the front yard area, while Officer Smith, flashlight in hand, went around to the back of the dwelling.

He rounded the side of the house checking for evidence of a forced entry. Now standing in the backyard, he proceeded to check each window along the back portion of the house and observed that all the windows were closed, except for one which was ajar about six inches. However, the open window was protected from the outside elements with a screen- closed and in good repair.

There was a tree located in the backyard, about 15 feet from the open window. It was here that Officer Smith found himself standing as an unusual light caught his attention.

The officer's observant senses alerted him to a strange, soft, white, luminous, glow originating from the dark room in which the window was ajar. It was at that moment something happened that he said: *"...I cannot explain to this day."*

In amazement, he watched as the source of the glow came into view. There, inside the darkened room, was a glowing ball or orb about the size of a tennis ball. Then, the glowing orb, slowly but steadily, proceeded to float out the open window, *"...right through the screen"*.

Unfazed by the metal sieve it had just passed through, it slowly and steadily continued on its way, about chest high, and headed towards the officer. Rather than collide with the policeman, its course veered and it slowly made two neat loops around the truck of the tree next to which Officer Smith was standing. Continuing on, it

headed towards the back of the property, and then just…
disappeared.

"It was the strangest thing that I have ever seen," said the police officer.

The officer explained that he was truly baffled, and started to run a mental list of possibilities through his mind. He ruled out the light from his or his partner's flashlight, or car headlights or someone from inside the dwelling as the source. The possibility that it was a reflection was also eliminated.

According to Officer Smith, there was not a burglary in progress, but the reason for the vacant house was a melancholy tale. An older couple had lived there and their son, now grown, had moved out of the area. A year and a half prior, the wife had died, leaving her husband a widower. The grieving husband's health soon failed and about 6 months before had also passed from this life into the next.

The unidentified vehicle belonged to the couple's son who lived out of state and returned to get the property ready for sale. Ironically, the day that Officer Smith got the call to investigate, it was the second anniversary date of the wife's death.

What was the strange ball of light that so peacefully floated out the window, past Officer Smith, as it defied the laws of gravity, and physics, and made several loops around a tree trunk and then disappeared? Officer Smith had no explanation then. Officer Smith has no explanation now.

For those of you who might doubt this story; you might be inclined to look it up in the record books, as law enforcement officials spend most of their time writing reports of the events that happened during their shift.

Do not bother. You will not find it.

Officer Smith calmly commented: *"I didn't write a report about that...who would believe it anyway..."*

Author's note: see page 87, "Balls of Light"

THE GHOST OF
QUEEN ANN HILL

"Mid pleasures and palaces though we may roam,

Be it ever so humble, there's no place like home"

J. Howard Payne

The following story has to be one of the most intriguing that I have ever heard. It brings to mind just how strong the pull of home is on the human spirit.

I have noticed over the years, that when one steadily approaches the final act of one's life, many find their thoughts are uncontrollably, pulled towards the memories of the place called home.

As Dorothy in the *Wizard of Oz*, no distance seems too great, and thousands of miles melt into none. Some have traveled across a continent; some have sailed across an ocean to visit the place of their longing. However, Mrs. Clark, about whom you are about to read, traveled from where many think none can - from beyond the grave.

Chere Resnick, of Laguna Nigel, California, told me her strange tale and wrote that it took her years before she could talk to anyone about her "Mrs.Clark".

In the early 1960's, Chere bought a home in an old section of Seattle, Washington called Queen Anne Hill.

Chere explained that Seattle is made up of seven hills and Queen Anne Hill overlooks Lake Union and in the far distance, one can see Lake Washington. The reason she pointed this geographic typography out to me, she explained, was that it was the breathtaking view that was the main reason for her interest in the home.

The house was an old two-story dwelling with large rooms, and a terrific view. It had a rather small back yard; the space of which was almost completely taken up by a huge, Royal Ann cherry tree.

The young couple that owned and lived in the house was anxious to sell, and as Chere explained, *"...(they) literally shoved the escrow papers in front of me."*

Along with selling the house below market value, the furniture and appliances went along with the purchase and Chere thought that she was very lucky!

That feeling lasted, for about three months after moving in. However, Chere started to think that maybe she was not so lucky, as she started to experience an unshakable feeling that someone was watching her. Of course, Chere lived there alone, but she had a "creepy" feeling that she could not explain. Then, other things began to happen.

Lights in the house would go on themselves. The stereo would go on suddenly. She thought that these problems indicated some kind of short in the old wiring system of the house. Concerned, she had an electrician check the house, but he assured her that the wiring was safe and operating properly.

It was then that she started to question herself. However, there was one specific room in the house, which she found most unsettling.

Along the back of the house was the master bedroom. It measured 32 feet long by 14 feet wide, with sliding glass doors that went to a lanai (deck) which extended out, and under a beautiful, Queen Ann cherry tree. One could stand on the lanai, reach up, and pick cherries.

Chere recalled that it was beautiful, but the only trouble was, every time she entered that room she became cold, and the little hairs on the back of her neck would stand on end. Unnerved by her reaction to the room, Chere moved her belongings upstairs to one of the other bedrooms, and for about a month even refused to go near the master bedroom.

One day, Chere, while at her weekly ladies' chat group, overheard a conversation. One of the ladies in the course of a conversation said that her brother was a medium. All the women that were there laughed, except for Chere.

Chere wanted to meet this man, so she intentionally invited him and his sister over for cake and coffee. Next, she intentionally guided him and his sister out to the lanai and cherry tree outside of the master bedroom.

Within five minutes, out came the brother who said to his sister, *"Let's go!"*

Almost uncontrollably, Cherie blurted out, *"...it's haunted, isn't it?"*

His reply was a short, simple, *"yes"*.

Chere pressed on, and asked him to tell her everything. The short time that the medium was in the room he learned a lot.

First, the ghost was a woman named Mrs. Clark; second, she wanted Chere to contact her two daughters who lived in southern Oregon and tell her daughters that she was fine; and third, she did not like the changes that Chere was making to her home.

Chere listened politely to this man, said goodbye, then promptly locked the door behind them as they left. Was this guy crazy...Chere had not purchased the house from a Clark?

Later that afternoon, Chere walked over to the neighbors. A small fence, separated the Lampkins' backyard from Chere's backyard and as nonchalantly as she could, Chere asked how long the Lampkins had lived in their home.

"Thirty years", was the reply.

"Well, I guess you have known all the people that have lived in this house," said Chere.

"Yes," said Mrs. Lampkin.

"Did you know the people who lived in the house prior to the couple I bought from?" asked Chere.

Mrs. Lampkin said, *"Oh...you mean the Clarks?"*

Chere nearly stopped breathing, and trying to remain calm, listened intently. Mrs. Lampkin went on to say that the Clarks had two daughters, but both of them moved away, and Mrs. Lampkin thought one of them had moved to a small town in northern Oregon. She also told Chere that the cherry tree, that filled Chere's backyard, was a gift from Mr. Clark to his bride.

The things that happened during the time Chere lived in her haunted home were indelibly etched into her memory. She says that she will never forget yelling at something that she could not see to get out of her house and to leave her alone. She actually considered calling a Catholic priest to exorcise the place.

Finally, Chere turned to the medium that she had invited for coffee and cake and as politely as she could, asked him if he knew how to rid the place of her uninvited houseguest.

The medium said that he did know how to get rid of the ghost, and told Chere to move out for three or 4 days.

Chere followed his advice, then moved back in a few days later. Lying in bed that evening, she was startled to hear someone downstairs crying. Investigating, she descended the stairs and found the sobbing was coming from the master bedroom. Opening the door, she peered inside only to find the room was empty. She made her way to the sliding glass doors, pushed them open and stepped out onto the lanai just as the neighbors, Mr. and Mrs. Lampkin, were making their way across the yard to her house. The Lampkins had heard the crying also, and had thought it was Chere crying. It was by this time that the crying had slowed and finally stopped.

Chere had had it. She packed her belongings, and started to get the house ready to sell. While busy in her quest to vacate her haunted environment, the telephone rang. It was Mrs. Lampkin.

"What did you do to the tree?" inquired Mrs. Lampkin.

"What tree?" asked Chere.

"The tree...the cherry tree..." was the response.

Chere made her way to the master bedroom and opened the drapes. There was her beautiful tree, completely black, no leaves, and this gooey stuff, like sap, running down the trunk.

The next week, a tree surgeon came to examine the tree and make a diagnosis.

"Lady...your tree is dead," he said.

"No kidding," thought Chere.

Speaking out loud now, Chere asked, *"Well, why...what happened to it?"*

"Sometimes it just happens", was the informed reply from the tree surgeon.

The next week, a crew came to saw down the dead cherry tree and haul it away. Chere and Mrs. Lampkin now stood in the yard, Chere on the spot where the beautiful tree once flourished.

"I wonder if we will ever know what happened to it," said Chere to Mrs. Lampkin as they surveyed the empty yard.

"I know what happened to it," said Mrs. Lampkin, in a soft, pensive voice, *"...Mrs. Clark took her tree with her when she left..."*

A FRIEND IN NEED

"Great truths are portions of the soul of man;
Great souls are portions of eternity."

James Russell Lowell
Sonnet vi.

How many of us have experienced the sound of our inner voice and taken heed and found we had, by just sheer chance, been snatched from the jaws of danger? The phenomenon is not rare, but rare is the person who slows the wheels of thought and listens.

It happened to my son just the other day. He had booked a flight to Washington DC, and planned to then travel on to Virginia. After he got off the phone, he walked into the room and said, *"Mom, I've got a bad feeling about that flight..."*

I was reading the newspaper and without skipping a beat, my immediate reply was, *"Cancel."*

He did. Sure enough, the next day, the television news reported an emergency landing at the Lancaster Airport, a flight out of Harrisburg International...smoke in the cockpit. It was Justin's cancelled flight.

Sometimes the event is not strictly precognition, but sometimes involves the help of one who may be thousands of miles distant, or even further away. I recall one such true event that was told to me by my English teacher when I was a freshman in high school.

Miss Roman explained to the class that while she was attending college and living in New York City, she landed a job that she really wanted. The first day that her job was to start, she returned home after classes and decided to take a little nap so she would be refreshed to show up that first day. She set the alarm and dozed off.

All of a sudden she felt someone grab both of her legs, pick them up and violently swing them off the couch, forcing her to sit straight-up, rudely awakened from a dead sleep.

Much to her shock and surprise, there standing in front of her was the transparent image of a woman, a stranger. Miss Roman blinked several times and tried to clear the sleep from her eyes; the woman disappeared into thin air.

Recovering her senses, she realized that she had slept through the alarm. She had only enough time to quickly dress and dart out the door. She was on time for the first day on the job.

Weeks later, while visiting her mother, Miss Roman described the strange woman who had so abruptly "threw" her off the sofa. Quietly her mother motioned her to follow her into the bedroom where she pulled a box out of the closet. Shuffling through the jumbled pile of photos, she pulled out an aged, yellowed picture of a woman, and showed it to Miss Roman.

Shocked, Miss Roman identified the woman as the one who awakened her. It was her grandmother who had died... a year before Miss Roman was born.

Chere Resnick, who owned the haunted house in Seattle, Washington (see page 54), also wrote to tell me about two other experiences that she had. The following occurrence she described as *"most profound"* and *"rather odd"*. I agree that it is profound, but not odd; I am pleased she agreed to let me share it with you.

It was during the mid-1960's; and the Vietnam War was raging thousands of miles away from the Seattle, Washington countryside. Many of Chere's friends were being drafted or joining the armed services, and of course, as soon as military basic training was completed, they were sent off to Vietnam to fight and die.

Chere had a brother named Mike, and her bother had a best friend, also named Mike. The two Mikes were the kind of friends who did everything together and, as Chere explained, they were inseparable.

Brother Mike found himself in military service and started out by doing office work for the military before he was sent to Vietnam. Friend Mike had no such reprieve, and almost immediately found himself in the rice paddies and jungles of a country half a world away. During this time, Chere explained that she had purchased a new car.

She remarked: *"...I was so proud of it..."*

One day, shortly after buying the new car, she decided to pack up her poodle and take off for the ocean.

"Ah...youth," Chere commented, as she recalled the start of her excursion.

She headed for the town of Westport located about a two and a half-hour drive from Seattle, Washington. It was a beautiful day as Chere breezed along the highway doing 60 miles an hour.

Chere explained further: *"I'm driving along at 60, when out of the clear blue sky, I hear my friend Mike's*

Figure 8 American soldiers do a land mine sweep somewhere in Vietnam in early 1968. Photo courtesy of Joseph Crouse.

voice say 'slow down Chere', *then he started to yell at me...*'slow down Chere!'.*"

Startled at hearing her friend Mike's voice, she was a bit rattled and slowed the car and took the next exit off the highway. Almost immediately, her right front tire blew out.

Chere was not only upset, about the strange voice of friend Mike, but also terrified that the tire could have blown out while she was doing 60 miles an hour, and she started crying. According to Chere, two nice teenage boys stopped and thought she was crying just about the flat tire, and changed the tire for her and got her on her way.

Well, Chere's trip to Westport was ruined, so she drove home. Her brother happened to be home at that time so, of course, he asked her what happened that she did not make it to Westport.

Chere told him about the blowout and then said, *"...if it hadn't been for Mike yelling at me to stop, I would have crashed."*

It was then that Chere's brother turned white as ash, and grabbed the back of the sofa to keep from falling. It was several moments, before her brother could speak.

Brother Mike gathered his composure and then told Chere that he had spoken to friend Mike's mother only that very morning. Mike was dead, killed in Vietnam the previous day.

Authors note: The next day, Chere took the tire to the local Goodyear dealer and asked why the tire had blown out. After doing all the tests that tire people do, they could find no cause for the tire failure.

MARY'S FLOWERS

"Too late I stayed,--forgive the crime!
Unheeded flew the hours;
How noiseless falls the foot of time
That only treads on flowers."

William Robert Spencer
Lines to Lady A. Hamilton

House hunting can be a most interesting experience. Each house one explores seems to have its own character, its own personal "feel", and then one comes across a dwelling that has no character at all. That house just sits there, like a very large…well, vegetable. Oh, it might have that extra bathroom, the garage one needs, plenty of cupboard space, or that beautiful flooring, but it lacks something that defies explanation. One could live there a hundred years and never feel at home.

That wasn't the case with the Kleckners from Landisville, Pennsylvania who had their eye on a little house located just a few doors down the street from where they lived. Thinking that the house would probably never go up for sale, they looked at houses on the market in the area. For two years, they searched, but each house they looked at left them disappointed.

"All I had to do was walk in the front door…it could have been beautiful inside…but it just was not the house for us…" explained wife and mother, Sandra Kleckner.

65

One day, Dick, Sandra's husband, walked down the street and passed the little brick, two-story home on the corner, the yard of which was filled with a profusion of flowers. His wife Sandra, had often commented how she loved the quaint, brick house, and often admired the explosion of scent and color as the butterflies flitted in and out of the garden.

There in the garden stood Mrs. Mary Mumma, just straightening up from digging in the rich, fertile beds. They waved a greeting to each other and had a friendly chat. It was then that Dick mentioned to Mary that if she ever decided to sell her home, that Sandra and he would really appreciate a chance to purchase it, as his wife, Sandra, loved the flowers.

One week later, Mrs. Mumma had a heart attack. She was a lovely woman and had lived in the house all her married life; in fact, her parents had built the home for her and her husband.

Tragically, Mary Mumma died. About one week after the funeral, Mary's son contacted Sandra and Dick Kleckner. He explained that his mother talked to him before her death and said that several people had expressed an interest in the house. It was his mother's wish that the Kleckners be given the first opportunity to buy the property.

Sandra and her family went over to the house and Mary's son showed them through. Nothing in the house had been touched since Mary's death, and the tour began in the attic.

Sandra recalls a comment her son, Marshall, made as they were walking down the attic steps: *"Mom, I feel like I've lived here all my life...."*

Sandra looked at him, surprised that his sentiments so closely resembled hers, nodded her head and added, *"So do I."*

The Kleckners purchased the house, moved in, and Sandra could hardly wait to get into the garden. Ignoring all the boxes that needed unpacked, Sandra made her way into the garden which was bursting with early summer blooms. It was a hot and humid afternoon, as Sandra kneeled in the beds surrounding the porch, her hands cooled by the moist soil as she weeded.

It was then that her concentration was interrupted by the sound of humming. It was a woman's voice, light, melodic, and happy. The sound was not constant, but intermittent; sometimes it was soft, sometimes it got louder.

Sandra looked around for the source of the singing but could find no one. She even got up off the ground, removed herself from her weeding, and walked around the house to investigate. Possibly, the neighbors might be out in the yard, but no one was there.

She was serenaded for the remainder of the time she spent in the garden that day. Pleased with all that she had accomplished by clearing the beds that surrounded the porch, she stopped for the day.

The next morning, Sandra stepped out onto the porch to admire the fruits of all her gardening of the previous day. Then she noticed something laying in the yard, alongside of the freshly weeded bed: an old and tattered pair of garden gloves.

"Where did they come from?" she wondered.

The gloves did not belong to Sandra; the gloves were not there yesterday, and she cleaned everything up, Sandra was positive about that.

Just then an old lady came walking down the street and paused to speak: *"Oh, you're working in Mary's garden...Mary loved her flowers. I can almost see her now with her old, worn out gloves, singing away..."*

Sandra became a little weak in the knees, as a strange feeling of cognition brightened her bewilderment.

"I believe that Mary worked along with me in the garden that day," explained Sandra, *"We have lived here since 1977, but it has always been Mary's garden."*

Over the years, numerous people have stopped to talk to Sandra as she tends the flowers. Most comment how happy Mary would be to know that Sandra takes such good care of the flowers.

Sandra remembers the incident in the garden with a smile, yet I watched tears well up in her eyes as she paused to contain the strong emotion , which after all these years, accompanies the recollection.

There is an explanation for Mary's return and Sandra summed it up very simply by saying, *"Mary's spirit was not settled or comfortable until she found out that the greatest love of her life was taken care of..."*

UPDATE:

THE HEADLESS HORSEMAN

"Tell me the tales that to me were so dear,
Long, long ago, long, long ago."

Thomas Haynes Bayly
"Long, long ago."

After I publish a book, it is not unusual for me to receive letters or telephone calls from readers who have additional information about the story. I have and will continue to include the additional information in each new publication.

THE HEADLESS HORSEMAN

This story first appeared in ***Haunted Lancaster County, Pennsylvania: Ghosts and Other Mysteries*** in 1994. The story has been around for so long that it could be classified as a "legend".

As the story goes, back in the 1800's a man, drinking in a tavern situated in the small village of Ironville, Lancaster County, Pennsylvania, knew he had to make the ride several miles back into the town of Columbia by midnight in order to save himself from the wrath of his "little woman". He was drunk as a lord when the clock read five minutes to midnight as he bolted out the door. His hasty departure was punctuated by yelling his final oath to his drinking buddies: *"I'll be in Columbia by the stroke of midnight, or I'll be in Hell..."*

Well, to make a long story short, as he got to the bend of the Ironville Pike around the small village of Norwood, his horse ran under a low hanging branch and the drunken rider was decapitated. (I guess one could say that he lost his head before getting back home to the wife.)

For decades there have been various reports from residents of Ironville and Norwood, that the sound of hoof beats is often heard at night and the event is sometimes accompanied by the sight of a headless rider.

James "Pud" H. Clark, of Hobe Sound, Florida, wrote to me to tell me that the story of the "Headless Horseman" jogged his memory about an event that happened to him many years ago. Mr. Clark, who lived in Columbia, Pennsylvania until 1940, and then again from 1945 to 1957, recalled the strange experience.

Mr. James "Pud" Clark and his friend, Ed Stair, who both lived in Columbia at the time, decided to camp out one night. After some thought, they decided to make their campsite on the edge of Wisler's woods, which was then located at the back end of Laurel Hill Cemetery.

The boys neatly spread their blankets and settled down for a peaceful night's sleep, when the sound and vibration of hoof beats startled them.

Mr. Clark explained what happened next:

"We jumped up and shone Ed's powerful five cell flashlight all through the woods. Seeing nothing, we decided that maybe Phil Glatfelter had passed by and we lay down again. Then we heard and felt the hoof beats again. Two thirteen year old boys (then) decided to vacate the area."

Mr. Clark further explained that he knew Phil Glatfelter very well, and the next time that he saw him, he told Mr. Glatfelter his story. According to Mr. Clark, Phil Glatfelter denied being in the area on that specific night.

Who was the rider on horseback that frightened two adolescent boys so many years ago? Was it really Phil Glatfelter, a local man known to ride his horse in the area?

Mr. Clark summed it up by writing:

"Maybe he was joshing an impressionable kid, but then again, maybe not..."

UPDATE:
Miss Mary Mifflin

*"And like a passing thought, she fled
In light away."*
Robert Burns
The Vision

T he story about the ghost of Miss Mary Mifflin was chronicled in my first book, *Haunted Lancaster County, Pennsylvania: Ghost and other Strange Occurrences* in 1994. Miss Mary lived in the small, rural village of Norwood, located outside the town of Columbia, Pennsylvania during the 1800's. The fair maid was the sister of Lloyd Mifflin, an artist, and sonneteer.

Mary, a young, red headed beauty, met with an untimely death in 1881 at the age of 18. Although the local newspapers of the day said her death was caused by an accidental shooting of her own hand; neighbors were more inclined to believe that it was suicide.

For years, there have been reported sightings of an ethereal figure of a young woman walking Norwood Road and the Ironville Pike, which run close to the standing, Mifflin family mansion. The witnesses are credible people, and the accounts though many times separated by time, are intriguingly similar.

In July of 1998, I received a telephone call from a woman who once lived next door to the old Mifflin Mansion, but requested her identity remain anonymous and so I will refer to her only as Miss Jones.

Miss Jones called after reading the story of Miss Mary and realized that Miss Mary might be the answer to a frequent, odd occurrence she witnessed several times, that transpired outside her apartment window.

The apartment house Miss Jones lived in, known as Cloverton, at one time, was part of the Mifflin estate. Over the years, the large house had several owners and was even used as a Catholic convent for some years. Eventually, it was turned into apartments and is still used as such.

The apartment which Miss Jones occupied was located on the second floor of the dwelling and on the east side of the house, her windows overlooking the former Mifflin Mansion and the small patch of woods that separated them. Miss Jones remarked that on several occasions during her stay in the apartment, she had glanced outside, around the evening hours, and noticed a woman, dressed in a long white dress, standing on the edge of the patch of forest.

Miss Jones commented:

"...I thought it was so weird...Why was she standing there?...I watched a good five minutes and she never moved...like staring off in a daze. I wondered why anyone would stand in a patch of woods with a white dress on...?"

According to Miss Jones, she saw the woman on several different occasions from the vantagepoint of her apartment window and each time the woman was wearing a white dress. The sightings were most often just before dusk.

Miss Jones explained that she only recently read my book and story about Miss Mary Mifflin; and the story struck her with an episode of déjà vu.

Did Miss Jones witness the phantom so many others have seen over the years along Norwood Road?

Maybe.

TRIPPER T. LOCKS: GHOST DOG

"But thinks, admitted to that equal stay,
His faithful dog shall bear him company."

Alexander Pope
Essay on Man

I ndeed, sometimes one tends to forget about the furry creature that shares one's life, and loves one unconditionally. I am guilty of that, for instance, I have a best friend, and her name is "Miss". It was only after I decided to tell this story that I realized that I too, had forgotten her.

Miss Winston, my tiger cat, has been at my side, through thick and thin, sickness and health, good times and bad, for 19 years. No better friend could one have.

To be accurate, when I told the story about my late husband (see page 9), I was remiss not to mention her. Really, she and I cared for my critically ill husband, as she never left his side, or my side, day or night, for those last 31 days. Three chairs were lined beside my husband's deathbed, at which our family of four kept watch. We sat in this order: son, wife, cat, and son. There were no questions about including her, and no complaints, as we shifted slightly to make room for one most faithful, who loved him, as did we. I watch her health fail now, as the years take their toll on her seven and a half-pound feline body, that sheds fur like a worn out mink coat; and I cannot help but wonder, what I will do without her.

Over the years, I have heard several accounts of owners seeing ghosts of their departed pets, but the following story has to be one of the most poignant.

Tripper T. Locks.

"A pedigree name for a pedigree dog," explained Roy King, formerly of Rheinholds, Pennsylvania and a current resident of Lebanon, PA.

Tripper was a gift to him on his 20th birthday in 1977. She was a mongrel dog that was found at the Humane Society in Lancaster, Pennsylvania; she was part German shepherd, part Labrador, and black as coal.

"Smartest dog I've ever had..." explained Mr. King, *"...almost human."*

In fact, she was so smart, the family taught her how to wave. Wave hello, wave goodbye, like Curly of the *Three Stooges*.

Seventeen years the family had with Tripper, through thick and thin, good times and bad. However, age took its toll and Tripper suffered a series of strokes.

"She dragged herself out of the house and into the garage...she didn't want to mess in the house, and that is where I found her – barely alive," said Roy King.

Mr. King and his youngest daughter took their beloved companion to the veterinarian. She was too sick and old to be helped and it was there, a member of the family, Tripper T. Locks, a human with fur, was put to sleep.

"We brought her body home, and my youngest daughter and I dug a grave in the front yard...we gently placed her in..." Mr. King recalled, as his eyes betrayed his painful memory.

Mr. king continued: *"I went into the house and asked Erin, our oldest daughter, if she wanted to come out and see Tripper and say goodbye for the last time before I filled in the hole...and she said 'I don't have to...I've already seen Tripper...'"*

Erin, who was about nine years old at the time, was standing in the kitchen. She told her father that she had turned around, looked through the screen door, and much to her amazement, saw Tripper T. Locks sitting on the porch...waving at her.

She then followed Tripper out to the garage where Tripper was now sitting. As Erin bent over to pet Tripper on the head; Tripper vanished into thin air.

Roy King says he truly believes that Erin saw Tripper. He does not doubt her story and fervently believes that Tripper came back to let Erin know that she was all right.

Over the site of Tripper's grave the Kings planted a Weeping Japanese cherry tree. Although they moved several years ago from the property where their beloved friend is buried, the loss of Tripper T. Locks left a very large hole in the hearts of the Kings.

"I've had many a dog over the years, but none, none, ever to compare to Tripper T. Locks...", said King,*"...smartest dog there ever was...smartest dog..."*

TOWER OF LONDON

*"I know death hath ten thousand several doors
For men to take their exit."*
John Webster
Duchess of Malfi. Act IV. Sc. 2

R ecently, while on maneuvers with the United States Navy, our son, Justin Dickinson had the opportunity to visit Great Britain. The ship pulled into Plymouth, England for a weeklong port visit over the July 4th American holiday in 1998.

The sailors had three days of liberty and so Justin and two friends, Jose and Ed, took a train into the city of London. They arrived at Paddington Station about 2:30 in the afternoon. Wanting to take in the sights the three men started walking all over London. Their stroll took them down to Buckingham Palace, Trafalgar Square, Hyde Park and being rather short on funds, the young men spent the evening looking for one of the cheapest hotels that they could find.

Exhausted from the previous day's trek, they decided to get a ticket on one of the many tour busses that crossed London on an hourly basis. The fellows rode around all day long, stopped at every tourist stop to see the sights, and took a great number of photographs.

Justin had one desire, because he just happened to be in London, England; he wanted to see the Crown Jewels. His companions, on the other hand, were not very enthused about going to see jewelry...they were after all, sailors. After much coaxing, Jose and Ed finally agreed to go see the jewels.

Now the fellows only had one problem, they did not know where the jewels were. Therefore, they began asking the tour guides.

It went something like this: *"Excuse me.... Sir, we want to go see the Crown Jewels...do you know where they are at?"*

The guide answered, *"They are in the Tower of London."*

To which Justin replied, *"Thanks...ah...by the way...where is the Tower of London?"*

The guide gave the fellows directions, and told them the correct bus to ride. They were on their way to find the jewels.

While riding the bus and soaking in the sights and jabbering away, Justin was overcome with a feeling of dread. It was at that moment, he looked out the bus window to his left, and spied a huge stone building which looked like a cross between a monastery and a castle.

Justin then turned to his friends and said, *"Hey, I don't know what that building is...but I am not going in there..."*

Jose and Ed looked at Justin as if he were crazy and asked what he meant. It was difficult for Justin to explain why the hair on his neck stood on end, or why he had such a compelling feeling that the looming stone structure was just a *"bad..."* place, but Justin explained the best he could.

"Ok, whatever...", they responded.

Figure 9 The Tower of London is where Britain's Crown Jewels are kept. Countless people were tortured, imprisoned, and died here. Guards say it is haunted and guard dogs will not enter the premises. Photo courtesy of Justin Dickinson, July, 1998.

It turned out that the stop that the guide told them to take happened to be right in front of the building. As the bus driver said: *"Tower of London,"* in his thick, English accent, Justin had a sinking feeling in the pit of his stomach.

It was then, the argument started, with Justin insisting he was absolutely not going to go into the building...Crown Jewels or not. For ten minutes the three argued. Justin only surrendered his will, *"against his better judgement"*, when his friends bribed him by paying for his admission to the tower.

They entered and toured the towers without incident. However, Justin, Jose, and Ed, spoke with the guards and asked if the place was haunted and if they had ever seen any strange things happen.

The tower guard explained that the tower is always under 24-hour guard and someone is constantly on watch protecting the jewels and roaming the grounds. The guard, personally, had had several experiences, one of which was hearing voices in rooms that were supposed to be empty. He added that some guards have experienced being choked, and or pushed, by an unseen assailant.

The tower was built by William the Conqueror and occupies the sight where the Romans built a fort almost 1000 years earlier. Traces of the Roman fort walls are still evident, and are incorporated into the present day structure. Over the centuries, countless men and women were tortured, imprisoned, and beheaded in this prison as executions were numerous.

The three men listened intently, fascinated by the tales of the tower. Jose and Ed, who had found Justin's reluctance to enter the building a topic for teasing, soon stopped their good-natured harassment after they heard the following fact.

Justin is not the only one who has refused to enter the Tower of London. According to the British guard that spoke to the men, there are no guard-dogs or watchdogs on the premises. Officials have tried to use canine guards, but no dog will enter the tower. The British have tried to employ these dogs for security. But much to their dismay, any dog released into the tower and or the tower grounds, would dig, scratch, and howl at the gates, or at which ever door blocked the dog's means of escape, until someone released the poor canine from his tower of terror.

The guards described the dogs as going "wild", and totally uncontrollable.

The subject of Justin's reluctance to enter that building was not discussed again. Jose and Ed must have been satisfied with Justin's rather accurate sixth sense.

Strange but true.

ACKNOWLEDGEMENTS

S eldom is one afforded the opportunity to publicly thank people for helping to make their life a little sweeter by taking some of the sting out of life's *"...arrows of outrageous fortune[31]"*.

Try, as one will, after the finished product has gone to press; inevitably, someone's name has been overlooked, but truly, not forgotten. Sometimes even the smallest kindness, though accepted and unacknowledged, helped to paint the day just a little brighter, the grass, just a little greener, the music, just a little sweeter.

Thank you Dr. Thomas J. Biuso for your house calls that brightened the very soul of my husband, Sam, and helped lighten my heart. Thank you also to all of Dr. "B's" office staff and his associate, Dr. LaCorte.

A heartfelt thanks you to Dr. Paul Russo and his staff at Memorial Sloane Kettering Cancer Center in New York. Not only did you give us skill and science, you gave us that which is priceless: hope.

Thank you to Dr. Peter DeGreen and his staff, and to Dr. K.G. Berkenstock.

A special thanks to Jessie Drey and all the staff at Hospice of Lancaster County who helped us in our hour of need and who continue to be a source of comfort. Words seem inadequate.

Thank you to my sister, Bette Crouse, who flew around our home and to our aid during Sam's illness as a "wing-ed angel"; no request too much to grant; no need of ours ignored nor unfilled, and each deed a gift of love.

To our sons, James William and Justin Salem, and daughters, Marci and Michelle: no finer children born, nor none so loved.

To Martin and Rita Williams, for loving thy neighbor: thank you Martin for your prayers that soothed the soul.

Thank you to Rick Fisher, Joan Barr, Cheri Resnick, Daniel MacDougall, James "Pud" Clark, Mark Nesbitt, John May and Bonnie Graybeal, Janet and Richard Groom II, George White, the staff at the Historical Society of York County, Pa., Margo Evans, Sondra Lehman, and the staff at Mack Printing Group.

I would like to give a special thank you to Chad Shaffer of Painesville, Ohio, who wrote to me about a strange event he experienced concerning his grandfather. Chad, although I did not include any events dealing with electronic voice phenomena or EVP in this book, I hope to include some stories in my next and your account will be included. I thank you for taking the time to write. I appreciate it.

I like to compare the good will of others, though oft times intangible, to that which softly, yet subtly leaves its mark.

Many times I have strolled through my garden and felt a soft flutter against my face; the sensation possessed the ability to produce a giggle, uplift a spirit, or provoke a smile where none was found.

The kind thoughts of others, whether in sentiment, word, or deed, also flit and flutter. They too, leave their mark, no matter how brief or soft and gentle the touch…as the dust from a butterfly's wing.

Thank you.

BALLS OF LIGHT

G host photographer, Rick Fisher, has seen the orbs that he photographs through the night vision scope many times.

He writes: *"I had shown a group of 15 people this (phenomena) while in Gettysburg; and they had confirmed that they had seen the same thing. At a later date, I had told Mark Nesbitt (author of the book series, Ghosts of Gettysburg) and he and I and another group of people witnessed the same thing (at Sach's Mill Bridge in Gettysburg). Mark was so thrilled (with the sighting) that I believe I am in his fifth book in a chapter discussing just that.*

I have also witnessed these balls of light in cemeteries. It is an unbelievable sight as I watch and wait for some type of explosion but there is nothing: no reflection of light or anything...just straight into the ground. We believe that cemeteries are portals and this is how the spirits travel from our world into theirs and from what I have seen this is quite true."

Rick Fisher is the president of the Pennsylvania Ghost Hunters Society. For more information about the organization, monthly meetings, workshops, and membership, or if you need an investigation, he can be contacted by writing or calling:

Rick Fisher
1528 Manor Blvd.
Lancaster, Pa 17603

(717) 871-8610

E-mail: **rfisher@redrose.net**

ALSO AVAILABLE FROM

FIEDEL PUBLISHERS

717 KINDERHOOK ROAD
COLUMBIA, PA 17512

PHONE: 717-684-4251   FAX: 717-684-4175

E-MAIL: kinderhook@desupernet.net

HAUNTED LANCASTER COUNTY, PENNSYLVANIA:
GHOSTS AND OTHER STRANGE OCCURRENCES
April 1994
ISBN # 0-9640254-0-X

TRUE GHOST STORIES OF LANCASTER COUNTY,
PENNSYLVANIA
October 1995
ISBN # 0-9640254-1-8

GHOSTS AND OTHER MYSTERIES
April 1997
ISBN # 0-9640254-2-6

To Order Additional Books

By writing to:

Fiedel Publishers
717 Kinderhook Road
Columbia, Pa 17512

Or E-mail:
kinderhook@desupernet.net

All titles are $6.99 a copy
Please include $1.50 postage for first book and .50 cents
for each additional book.

*PA residents please add 6% sales tax.

About The Author

Dorothy Burtz Fiedel was born in Columbia, Pennsylvania. She graduated cum laude from Millersville University, Millersville, PA with a Bachelor of Science degree. She is the mother of two sons and grandmother of three.

ENDNOTES

[1] Kübler-Ross, Elisabeth. *Death the Final Stage of Growth*. Prentice-Hall, Inc., Englewood, New Jersey. 1975. P.2

[2] Ibid.

[3] Barker, George E. *Death and After Death*. University Press of America, Inc., 1979. P.52

[4] Osis, Karlis and Haraldsson, Erlendur. *At the Hour of Death* Avon Books. The Hearst Corporation. 1977. P.20

[5] Ibid.
[6] Ibid.
[7] Ibid.
[8] Ibid.
[9] Ibid.

[10] Head, Joseph and Cranston, S.L., eds. *Reincarnation the Phoenix Fire Mystery*. Julian Press/Crown Publishers, Inc., New York, New York. 1977. P.559

[11] Fodor, Nandor. *Encyclopaedia of Psychic Science*. University Books,Inc. 1966. P. 82

[12] Osis, Karlin and Haraldsson, Erlendur. *At The Hour of Death*. Avon Books. The Hearst Corporation. 1977.

[13] Heschel, Abraham J. *Prophetic Inspiration after the Prophets: Maimonides and Other Medieval Authorities*. Ktav Publishing House, Inc., Hoboken, NJ. 1996. P.23, 24

[14] Davis, Avrohom, Kornfeld, Nachum Y., and Walzer, Abraham B. *Healing and Deliverance: A Collection of Psalms and Prayers in*

Times of Illness. Typography by Simcha-Graphic Associates. Brooklyn, NY. 1993. P5-19

[16] Wilt, Jinny. "Accomac Inn", *The York Dispatch*, 1 July 1996.

[17] Ibid.

[18] Campbell, Douglas H. *Accomac Inn History*. 19 July 1993.

[19] Ibid.

[20] Kitman, Marvin. *George Washington's Expense Account*. Harper and Row, Publishers, Inc. New York, New York. 1970. P255.

[21] *The Picket Post*. Issued quarterly by Valley Forge Historical Society, Valley Forge, Pa. November 1957. P4.

[22] Campbell, Douglas. P3

[23] Diner, Phantom. "Back At The Accomac", *Central PA*. WITF, Inc., Harrisburg, Pa. October 1998.

[24] Lehman, Garry. "Murder At Coyle's Ferry". Manuscript in files of Historical Society of York, PA.

[25] Ibid.
[26] Ibid.
[27] *The York Gazette*. 29 April 1884.
[28] Ibid.
[29] Ibid.
[30] Ibid.
[31] Shakespeare, William. *Hamlet*